# Bosom
# Buddies

# Bosom Buddies

## A CELEBRATION OF FEMALE FRIENDSHIPS THROUGHOUT HISTORY

by VIOLET ZHANG    illustrated by SALLY NIXON

**CHRONICLE BOOKS**

SAN FRANCISCO

Library of Congress Cataloging-in-Publication data is available.

ISBN 978-1-4521-6839-5

Manufactured in China.

Design by Allison Weiner

10 9 8 7 6 5 4 3 2 1

Chronicle books and gifts are available at special quantity discounts
to corporations, professional associations, literacy programs, and
other organizations. For details and discount information, please
contact our corporate/premiums department at corporatesales@
chroniclebooks.com or at 1-800-759-0190.

Chronicle Books LLC
680 Second Street
San Francisco, California 94107
www.chroniclebooks.com

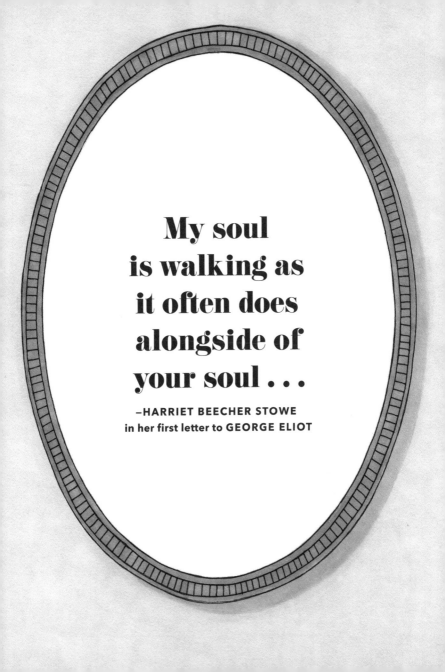

**My soul is walking as it often does alongside of your soul . . .**

–HARRIET BEECHER STOWE
in her first letter to GEORGE ELIOT

# Table of Contents

# Introduction

The term *bosom buddies*, meaning best friends, originated in the sixteenth century. The bosom was, at the time, considered a symbol of thoughtfulness and deep feeling. So in turn, a bosom buddy (or a bosom friend, as they said back then) was someone with whom you could share all your most private thoughts; someone you were very attached to emotionally. It's this kind of intimacy that you'll see in the friendships featured in this book.

From entertainment and sports to politics and activism, every woman in this book is the (s)hero of her own story, and worthy of her own praise. But, despite being spectacular as individuals, these leading ladies didn't do it alone; they had their besties beside them. Angela Davis and Toni Morrison merged literature and activism. Venus and Serena Williams took over the tennis world and crushed stereotypes about the game. Together, Qiu Jin and Xu Zihua, members of the Chinese literati during the Qing dynasty, rebelled against an unjust government. In times of stress and confusion, these women turned to one another for inspiration, advice, or simply comfort. They motivated each other to be better in their work, and stuck with one another through ups and downs, successes and failures.

Of course, these friendships weren't all rainbows and sunshine and butterflies. (What friendship is?!) Like any serious relationship, there was often tension and conflict—and in some cases even rivalry. Tennis idols Martina Navratilova and Chris Evert were best friends in their personal lives, but they destroyed each other on the court. Virginia Woolf and Katherine Mansfield connected on their writing, but were also deeply envious of one another. Zora Neale Hurston and Marjorie Kinnan Rawlings respected each other as writers, but their relationship was tainted by the racial prejudices of their time. This book explores those complicated aspects of friendship, on top of all the feel-good lovey stuff.

So get ready for hearty laughs with Tina Fey and Amy Poehler, a journey to the White House with Michelle Obama and Valerie Jarrett, and some serious political upheaval realness with the Trung sisters. The BFFs in this book prove that when smart, talented, motivated, and charismatic women get together, they are unstoppable.

And when you're finished reading this book, pass it on to the special women in your own life. Be inspired to unlock the power of your own bosom friendships.

# Trung
# Sisters

### TRUNG TRAC & TRUNG NHI

In the first century C.E., Vietnam was ruled by the Chinese Han dynasty. The Chinese government forced local leaders to report to the government and made Vietnamese people assimilate to Chinese culture: the Vietnamese were forced to adopt the Chinese language, beliefs in Daoism and Confucianism, Chinese customs, and even Chinese clothing.

The Trung sisters, Trung Trac and Trung Nhi, rebelled against the Chinese overlords in 40 C.E. and led what would be the first major Vietnamese rebellion against Chinese rule. The

older sister, Trung Trac, was married to a prominent local leader who was plotting a resistance against the Chinese when he was found out and subsequently assassinated. Despite the clear danger involved, Trung Trac decided to continue what her husband had started, and her little sister Trung Nhi joined her. The legend goes that in order to prove themselves and receive support from their community, the Trung sisters killed a tiger and wrote a proclamation of independence on the tiger's skin.

With local leaders and other armed sympathizers, the sisters marched through northern Vietnam, driving the Chinese away. Their army included many women—thirty-six of whom were generals, including the sisters' own mother. They eventually gained sixty-five citadels and established an independent Vietnamese kingdom located between southern China and present-day Hue, a city in central Vietnam. The sisters declared themselves the queens of this new state.

Sadly, their time as royalty didn't last long. After about three years, it became apparent that the resistance was unsustainable. They had few supplies left, they weren't getting a lot of support from the locals, and they didn't have the trained military personnel that they needed to keep fighting. And yet, despite all of this, the revolution persisted; the sisters carried on. They never formally surrendered, even when it was clear after multiple lost battles that the Chinese were going to win. Many accounts say that rather than admitting defeat to their enemy, the sisters chose instead to commit suicide by drowning in a river.

Today, there are many physical reminders of the sisters' service, including two pagodas and an avenue in Ho Chi Minh City named in their honor. But their greatest legacy is their spirit of resistance. Throughout the French invasion and the Vietnam War, the sisters were a source of inspiration for the Vietnamese people. Even today, soldiers often carry images of the sisters for encouragement. The Trung sisters are exemplary figures in Vietnamese history, viewed as models of strength and defiance in the name of justice.

**All the male heroes bowed their heads in submission; Only the two sisters proudly stood up to avenge the country.**

—Fifteenth-century poem

# Anne & Mary
### HUTCHINSON
### DYER

Anne Hutchinson joined the Massachusetts Bay Colony in 1634 and quickly became known in the community for hosting weekly spiritual get-togethers at her house. In these gatherings, Anne encouraged her fellow Puritans to share their ideas about faith and develop their own thoughts regarding theology. She encouraged personal religious freedom, where the individual is allowed to explore his or her own faith and relationship with God, without the need of a clergy. Many in the community took to this idea, and it wasn't long before Anne had a substantial following.

*Anne Hutchinson (left), Mary Dyer (right)*

Ironically and hypocritically—since the Puritans left England to *escape* religious persecution—the leaders of the Massachusetts Bay Colony had a problem with this. Pastor and Governor John Winthrop was not happy at all, and in a fit of character assassination, he turned the community against Anne by accusing her of blasphemy. Anne, steadfast in her beliefs, was tried before a general court and banished from the colony.

Mary Dyer, who held the same spiritual beliefs as Anne, chose to leave the church after Anne was excommunicated. Anne had been Mary's friend and midwife, and had been there for Mary when she went into premature labor. Unfortunately, the baby was stillborn with extreme deformities, which spread rumors that Mary had birthed a demon. Governor Winthrop had demanded the baby be dug up from the grave and had described it to the public as a monstrous creature with scales and claws. Needless to say, Mary had her own issues in the colony, and it wasn't long until she, too, was banished.

Both women lived in Rhode Island for a while before eventually parting ways. Following the death of her husband, Anne moved to what is presently New York. Unfortunately, she was killed there in an attack. Meanwhile, Mary moved back to England, where she joined the Society of Friends and formally became a Quaker. She had finally found her people! The Quakers also believed in the individual's ability to connect with God. In this community, Mary continued practicing the beliefs that Anne had imparted to her.

Mary eventually returned to the colonies to protest anti-Quaker laws. Seen as radical, she was arrested many times between 1658 and 1660, and was even banished *again* from Boston before being put on trial and sentenced to death.

Today, both women are remembered for their courage in defying a corrupt system—and for sticking together in their fight for religious freedom.

**Nay, I came to keep bloodguiltiness from you, desiring you to repeal the unrighteous and unjust law made against the innocent servants of the Lord. Nay, man, I am not now to repent.**

—MARY DYER

# Abigail ADAMS & Mercy OTIS WARREN

Abigail Adams is mostly known in American history as the second First Lady and wife of President John Adams. Lesser known is her deep friendship with Mercy Otis Warren, a prominent writer and political activist during the American Revolution. Abigail and Mercy met through their husbands, who ran in the same political circle in Massachusetts. The two women quickly developed their own relationship, a lot of which was explored through written correspondence.

*Abigail Adams (left), Mercy Otis Warren (right)*

The friends wrote to keep each other company while their husbands were away, which occurred increasingly often leading up to and during the revolution. Already an established author at the time, Mercy used her voice publicly. She had many published works, including plays, poetry, and political commentary. Abigail, on the other hand, limited her voice to a more private sphere, sharing her ideas in letters to her husband and friends. The two women wrote one another prolifically, discussing everything from family to politics to philosophy.

Mercy, the older of the two, took a preachy, big-sister tone in her communication with Abigail, but this didn't seem to bother Abigail, who was happy to be a pupil to her older friend. Abigail would turn to Mercy for advice or sometimes just to vent. In a now famous letter, Abigail asked her husband to "remember the ladies" and implored him to fight for women's rights. In response, John Adams called her "saucy" and ignored his wife's request. Upset by this, Abigail unleashed her anger about the situation to Mercy. Unfortunately, there's no record of Mercy specifically responding to *this* letter. Whether Mercy chose to ignore the issue or just never received the letter, we will never know. However, history shows Mercy to be a woman ahead of her time in many ways, often writing about military history and discussing politics.

Though they provided each other with solid companionship, the friends also encountered problems. A recurring one had to do with letter-writing etiquette. They frequently discussed in their letters who owed whom a letter, who cared about whom more—showing that perhaps neither felt totally secure in their relationship. They would later have a huge falling out after Mercy, a staunch anti-federalist, published a three-volume history titled *History of the Rise, Progress, and Termination of the American Revolution* that bashed John Adams for his political beliefs and claimed that he'd lost touch with the roots of the revolution. The friends eventually made up and continued writing to one another, though never as fervently as before. Their written correspondence spanned thirty years, from the time they met until Mercy's death.

# The balm of life, a kind and faithful friend.

–MERCY OTIS WARREN

If particular care and attention is not paid to the ladies, we are determined to foment a rebellion, and will not hold ourselves bound by any laws in which we have no voice or representation.

—ABIGAIL ADAMS in a letter to her husband JOHN ADAMS

# Brontë Sisters

**CHARLOTTE, EMILY & ANNE**

Charlotte, Emily, and Anne Brontë were born in Yorkshire County, England, and showed literary promise from a young age. Born only two years apart from one another—Charlotte first in 1816, then Emily in 1818, then Anne in 1820—the sisters were close and bonded over their shared love of stories. They had unlimited access to their father's library, and it was there, surrounded by books, that the seeds of imagination were planted.

*Brontë sisters: Emily (left), Anne (middle), Charlotte (right)*

Left alone together, the sisters spun lavish tales set in fantasy kingdoms, and compiled these stories in little notebooks, writing everything down in tiny, *tiny* script. The talent and attention to detail they showed as precocious children characterized their later works, first in their early twenties when they published a collection of poetry at their own expense (the struggle was real), and later on, in their novels.

What people often don't know is that Charlotte, Emily, and Anne were originally published under male pseudonyms. At the time, people weren't interested in female voices, so the sisters went by the pen names Currer, Ellis, and Acton Bell in order to give their work a fair shot in the world. Today, these sisters have a permanent place in the literary canon. Their books, the most famous of which are *Jane Eyre* (Charlotte) and *Wuthering Heights* (Emily), are discussed in high school and college classrooms around the world.

If we would build on a sure foundation in friendship, we must love friends for their sake rather than for our own.

–CHARLOTTE BRONTË

# Susan

#### B. ANTHONY

# & Elizabeth

#### CADY STANTON

The famous feminist friendship between Susan B. Anthony and Elizabeth Cady Stanton began in 1851 at an antislavery meeting in Seneca Falls, New York, where the two women met for the first time. Elizabeth and a few colleagues had hosted the women's rights convention in the same city just three years prior. It was there that Elizabeth presented the Declaration of Rights and Sentiments, a document she wrote proclaiming the social injustices against women. Susan also came from a background in reform. She was a temperance activist who urged wives to acquire legal

*Susan B. Anthony (left), Elizabeth Cady Stanton (right)*

counsel in situations where poverty or domestic violence was the result of their husbands' alcoholism.

With Elizabeth as the voice and ideologue and Susan as the campaign driver, the friends blazed the trail for what would be a long and hard fight for women's right to vote. Elizabeth was a writer and a thinker; Susan was an organizer and a doer. Their talents complemented each other perfectly, making the pair a force to be reckoned with.

The friends chased their mission with urgency and shattered multiple layers of the glass ceiling along the way. During the Civil War, they formed the Women's Loyal National League, the first national political organization for women. Five thousand women from the league gathered four hundred thousand signatures to persuade Congress to pass the Thirteenth Amendment abolishing slavery. For a while, the friends published a radical women's rights newspaper called *The Revolution*. Later in their careers they faced a major obstacle when they took a strong stance in favor of universal suffrage as opposed to suffrage first for black men, which many of their abolitionist friends believed was more urgent in the quest toward progress. These conflicting views caused friction in the suffrage movement. In 1890, the friends created the National American Woman Suffrage Association (NAWSA), for which Elizabeth served as president. In 1902, the friends organized an international conference of women, which proved to be the largest conference of its time. When Elizabeth retired from the NAWSA, Susan took over the position.

Though closely connected ideologically, the friends were physically apart for much of their careers. Both traveled a lot to give lectures, and because she didn't have a husband or kids, Susan was more often the one campaigning on-site. Meanwhile, Elizabeth was home working on personal writing projects. When the friends were apart, they wrote to one another in witty back-and-forth banter, showing that there was an openness to their friendship, an intimacy that allowed the two friends to be extremely honest with one another while maintaining a level of mutual respect.

Elizabeth died in 1902, and Susan passed away in 1906— only weeks after she gave her last speech at the NAWSA convention in Baltimore. Although the Nineteenth Amendment granting women the right to vote wouldn't pass for another fourteen years, Elizabeth and Susan inspired sister suffragettes everywhere to continue fighting the good fight. Even today, their legacy persists and they remain symbols of steadfastness and determination.

It is fifty-one years since we
first met, and we have been
busy through every one of
them, stirring up the world to
recognize the rights of women.
We little dreamed when we
began this contest, optimistic
with the hope and buoyancy
of youth, that half a century
later we would be compelled
to leave the finish of the bat-
tle to another generation of

women. But our hearts are filled with joy to know that they enter upon this task equipped with a college education, with business experience, with the fully admitted right to speak in public—all of which were denied to women fifty years ago. They have practically one point to gain— the suffrage; we had all.

—SUSAN B. ANTHONY in a letter to ELIZABETH CADY STANTON

# Mary &

TODD LINCOLN

# Elizabeth

KECKLEY

Despite coming from completely different backgrounds, Mary Todd Lincoln, wife of President Abraham Lincoln, and Elizabeth Keckley, the first lady's dressmaker, developed an authentic yet complicated friendship.

Elizabeth Keckley was born into slavery in Saint Louis, Virginia. She learned to sew at a young age from her mother, who had been the slave-owner's family's seamstress. Elizabeth endured severely cruel treatment until she was able to buy her and her son's freedom. She then made

*Mary Todd Lincoln (left), Elizabeth Keckley (right)*

her way north to Washington, D.C., where she opened a dressmaking shop. Her dresses were gorgeous, but a large part of Elizabeth's success was due to her business acumen. She had the entrepreneurial instincts to network and self-promote, and before long, she was the most coveted dressmaker among the white high society.

Around the time of President Lincoln's first inauguration, Elizabeth's fame landed her a job as personal dressmaker for Mary Todd Lincoln. A woman who loved shopping and fashion, Mary's initial interest in Elizabeth was purely professional, but as the two women started spending more time together (this is pre-mass production, so dresses took A LOT longer to make), the relationship took on a private dimension. Elizabeth became more than just a dressmaker for Mary—she became Mary's friend.

Devastatingly, both women's sons died young, and the friends turned to one another for comfort amidst this shared grief. Many accounts detail Elizabeth's loyal presence during Mary's hard time. She stayed with Mary throughout the Civil War and her husband's difficult presidency. Elizabeth was Mary's comfort and confidante, and on the fateful day of President Lincoln's assassination, it was Elizabeth's presence that Mary asked for.

Though her position as the first lady's dressmaker is Elizabeth's most enduring legacy, Elizabeth also had a life outside of that. She continued making dresses for other women, her business expanding so much that she had to hire seamstresses to work for her. As an active part of the free black community, Elizabeth established the Contraband Relief Association in 1862 and served as its president. The organization raised funds for food, clothes, and other necessities that went toward helping impoverished ex-slaves. Mary, one of the first to advocate for her friend, made a two-hundred-dollar donation. That's the equivalent of almost six thousand dollars today!

Unfortunately, this friendship did not last forever. Mary's frequent mood swings put pressure on the relationship, but what ultimately ended things was Elizabeth's memoir, *Behind the Scenes*, in which she revealed many details of the Lincolns' private lives. Elizabeth would write many letters to her friend apologizing, but their bond was never rekindled. Elizabeth later made a quilt from the scraps she'd saved from making Mary's dresses.

I consider you my best living friend.

–MARY TODD LINCOLN
in a letter to
ELIZABETH KECKLEY

# George & Harriet

ELIOT

BEECHER STOWE

American novelist Harriet Beecher Stowe first wrote to George Eliot, a British novelist, in 1869. The letter was spontaneous, apropos of nothing as far as anyone could tell, except perhaps a genuine desire to connect with another female writer. Both women were already well-established in their careers when their correspondence began. Harriet had risen to the height of fame with the publication of *Uncle Tom's Cabin*, a novel about the horrors of slavery that many believe catalyzed the Civil War. George (given name: Mary Ann Evans) had five novels

*George Eliot (top), Harriet Beecher Stowe (bottom)*

published by the time Harriet made first contact. Her most famous work, *Middlemarch*—widely regarded as the greatest novel in the English language—was still in progress.

Harriet's initial letter was both sincere and tactful; she seemed to *really* want this friendship and so, put in her best effort to charm and impress George. She provided a thorough analysis of George's work—showing she had read it carefully—both praising the work and giving literary suggestions. Next, she touched on the similarities that she and George shared as female writers. Finally, Harriet ended the letter by inviting George to visit her in the United States. In her letter back to Harriet, George thanked the American writer for her kind words.

Throughout the years, these women would exchange many thoughts and ideas. They developed a closeness that was largely unaffected by the two years of silence that would occur four times during their eleven-year relationship. Harriet would often disclose insecurities about her writing and George would offer encouragement. As she did in her initial letter, Harriet would continue to generously praise and also critique George's work—sometimes bluntly. One of her main critiques was that George's writing was overly intellectual and did not dwell enough on matters of the heart. She called George's work "artistic," but remarked that it was not for the masses to enjoy. This illustrates the stylistic differences between these two writers, for it was Harriet's style to write in more simple, conversational prose.

Not totally unrelated to her comments about feeling, Harriet would also repeatedly probe George on the subject of religion. Though both women rejected the dogmatic Evangelicalism that they'd been raised in, they forged wholly different spiritual paths. Harriet believed in the teachings of Jesus and the morality laid out in the Bible; George, meanwhile, rejected religion completely. Harriet tried many times to have discussions with George on religion, but to no avail. George wasn't interested and simply didn't engage Harriet on this point.

But George was one to push social boundaries. She was known for having premarital sexual relations with prominent men—a few of whom were married! Blatantly disregarding social convention, she had even lived with a married man named George Henry Lewes for twenty-four years.

Harriet and George maintained this pen-pal friendship until George's death in 1880. Though they never met, they often fantasized about it in their letters to one another.

Dear friend,—It is two years nearly since I had your last very kind letter, and I have never answered, because two years of constant and severe work have made it impossible to give a drop to anything beyond the needs of the hour. Yet I have always thought of you, loved you, trusted you all the same, and read every little scrap from your writing that came to hand.

–HARRIET BEECHER STOWE in a letter to
GEORGE ELIOT

# Qiu Jin & Xu Zihua

Xu Zihua was born into a scholarly family during the Qing dynasty. Surrounded by relatives who were poets or otherwise connoisseurs of poetry, Xu Zihua soon developed her own taste for the humanities. She read and wrote a lot of poetry throughout her childhood, and as an adult, she channeled her passion for literature into teaching. She became the principal at the Xunxi Girls' School, where she would eventually meet Qiu Jin, a fellow writer and teacher at the school.

*Xu Zihua (left), Qiu Jin (right)*

Qiu Jin's upbringing was similar to Xu Zihua's in that she was encouraged to read and received a solid education. As an adult, Qiu Jin studied in Japan and had views about womanhood that were unconventional for her time. She was against the tradition of foot-binding and thought that the Chinese family structure was oppressive to women. She wrote poems about female heroes and often wore men's clothes.

Bonded initially by their shared love of poetry, these women quickly found that they enjoyed talking to each other about many other topics of cultural significance, including politics and women's issues. Xu Zihua was greatly influenced by Qiu Jin's revolutionary ideas and was a huge support to Qiu Jin as she began expressing her views during China's political upheaval. At the time, many intellectuals in the country were frustrated with the government, which they viewed as incompetent. Encouraged by Xu Zihua, Qiu Jin started *Zhongguo Nü Bao*, a monthly newspaper for Chinese women. Qiu Jin also organized an uprising against the Qing leadership, which Xu Zihua and her sister helped fund by selling their jewelry.

Sadly, Qiu Jin was executed for this rebellion, her body buried haphazardly by the government. It was Xu Zihua (others were too afraid of the government) who relocated Qiu Jin to a proper burial site and arranged a funeral.

Xu Zihua honored her friend by founding the Qiu Society, the purpose of which was to commemorate Qiu Jin. To this end, Xu Zihua wrote numerous essays about Qiu Jin's life. It would seem that Qiu Jin's influence on Xu Zihua persisted beyond Qiu Jin's death, for Xu Zihua remained engaged in political activism. She became a prominent member of the Nanshe (Southern society), an activist literary group, and following the 1911 revolution that overthrew the Qing dynasty and established China as a republic, Xu Zihua started the Jingxiong Women's School in Shanghai. The name "Jingxiong," which means "Hero's Rival," was one of Qiu Jin's courtesy names (a name given to someone in adulthood). When Xu Zihua retired from the school in 1927, she handed the reins over to Qiu Jin's daughter.

Don't say
women can't
do heroic things
As I am about
to sail out for a
long journey
Alone on the
stormy East
Sea!

—QIU JIN

# Virginia & Katherine

WOOLF

MANSFIELD

Scholars have long been fascinated by the relationship between Virginia Woolf and Katherine Mansfield, which toggled between profuse admiration and subtle disdain. Katherine was born into the middle class while Virginia's family was part of the British intelligentsia, which included key artistic and political figures of the time. Despite these different backgrounds, Virginia and Katherine were alike in many ways. They were both writers with editor husbands, and both were without children. But their greatest similarity was their passion for writing. They both wanted to subvert

*Virginia Woolf (left), Katherine Mansfield (right)*

literary traditions and create fiction that took on new forms. It was this shared ambition that often caused tension in the friendship, creating a duplicitous aspect within it.

The two women met in the fall of 1917. At the time, Virginia was just coming into her own literary style, and hadn't written any of her major novels yet. Katherine, on the other hand, was already an established writer. A bond was formed out of mutual admiration. Virginia looked up to Katherine and her success, and Katherine acknowledged that Virginia was immensely talented, even though she was just starting out. In their letters to one another and to other people, both women expressed that they were happy to find solace and comfort in another person who understood their literary intentions—but it was also clear in these letters that they measured themselves against one another. Many scholars believe that this mutual jealousy is what motivated each woman to continually improve their work. (For you *Gilmore Girls* fans out there, they were the original Rory Gilmore and Paris Geller!)

To give you an idea of their feelings for each other, in a letter to a friend, Virginia wrote that Katherine stinks like "a civet cat that had taken to street walking." In another letter, Katherine begrudged Virginia her privileges, which Katherine believed provided Virginia a better foundation for good writing.

Though a lot of research has been done on their relationship and its effects on their writing, the friendship between Virginia and Katherine was sadly short-lived. It lasted only six years, from 1917 to 1923, the year Katherine died of tuberculosis. In the end, the friendship pushed each woman to greater heights and was key to their success as writers. Critics have said that while the women were already good writers when they met, the work that Virginia and Katherine created during the beginning of their friendship—"Kew Gardens" and "Prelude," respectively, both short stories—showed the women achieving the innovative and experimental methods that they had set out to tackle.

**You are
the only woman
with whom I long
to talk work.
There will never
be another.**

–KATHERINE MANSFIELD in a letter to
VIRGINIA WOOLF

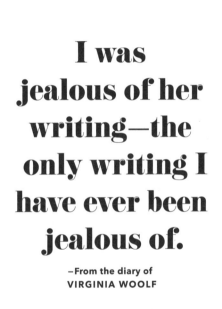

**I was jealous of her writing—the only writing I have ever been jealous of.**

–From the diary of
VIRGINIA WOOLF

# Anna & Marina

AKHMATOVA

TSVETAEVA

In this friendship between renowned twentieth-century Russian poets Anna Akhmatova and Marina Tsvetaeva, Marina made the first move. Already living abroad at the time, Marina decided to dedicate a cycle of eleven poems to Anna and send her the manuscript—even though the two had never met. It was a bold move, the intention of which was to humble herself; like a preemptive truce, the letter was meant to show Anna that Marina was *not* her competitor! Anna was so touched by this gesture that she carried the manuscript around with her in her handbag

*Marina Tsvetaeva (left), Anna Akhmatova (right)*

until the papers disintegrated. For years after that, the women would keep up a correspondence through letters and more dedications to one another, and Marina would even pop up occasionally in Anna's poems. Marina would keep one of Anna's letters with her at all times.

While this friendship was blossoming, Russia was in a state of turmoil. The Russian Revolution in 1917 destroyed czarist rule. Immediately afterwards, civil war broke out as many political parties fought over leadership of the new Russia. This lasted for five years and eventually led to the establishment of the Soviet Union in 1922. This was followed by the Great Purge, an effort led by Stalin to seek out and eliminate anyone who had ties to the Old Bolsheviks (the prominent party in Russia prior to the Russian Revolution). Many of the accused were tortured, sent to prison camps, and executed.

It was this social and political unrest that made Marina leave the country in 1922. After her daughter died during the Russian famine, Marina moved first to Berlin and then Prague before finally settling down in Paris, where she and her family lived in poverty. Writing sustained her, and she wrote and published many volumes of poetry during this lonely and difficult time. Her work was passionate, known for its staccato rhythms and the portrayal of women's experiences.

While Marina was abroad, Anna stayed in Russia—where her work challenged and upset the Soviet government. Due to the sophisticated language and emotional themes, the Communist party deemed her work "bourgeois" and first banned reading it from 1925 to 1940, and then banned publishing it in 1945. Anna also didn't shy away from writing about the horrors of Stalin's reign, which incited others to call her a "harlot-nun" and ostracize her from the Soviet writing community.

Anna and Marina finally met in 1940, when Marina returned to Moscow. They met up two days in a row and chatted for most of those days. Tragically, Marina hung herself only a year later, after her husband was executed and her daughter was sent to a labor camp. Anna was fortunate to live a longer life, but one still filled with strife. In 1950, she wrote poems praising Stalin in order to get her son out of prison (she would later request that these not appear in her collected works). But in 1958, after Stalin's death, Anna reemerged into the literary scene and began publishing real work again. One of her most notable poems, "Poem Without a Hero," was dedicated to Stalin's victims. Anna died at age seventy-six, adored by the Russian people for her courage.

Although these two women met only briefly, their bond with one another withstood the physical distance that separated them, and kept them afloat through difficult and painful periods. Though their friendship was ultimately insufficient to make up for the suffering they endured, the companionship they gave to one another was irreplaceable for as long as the bond lasted.

Today together Marina,
we walk in the capital
at midnight
And behind us there are
millions alike
And there is no
procession more somber
With the sad tolls
And Moscow's wild
moans
Of the snowstorm which
covers our tracks

—ANNA AKHMATOVA

# Zora & Marjorie

NEALE HURSTON

KINNAN RAWLINGS

Zora Neale Hurston and Marjorie Kinnan Rawlings shared an intimate yet unusual friendship. They met at the pinnacle of their careers in 1942, when Marjorie spoke at a college event that Zora was hosting. Just a few years prior, Zora had published *Their Eyes Were Watching God* (1937) and Marjorie had published *The Yearling* (1938), for which she won a Pulitzer Prize. Thematically, their novels shared similarities. Both were set in Florida and explored the lives and struggles of ordinary people. For both writers, setting was a huge part of their storytelling, and each woman had

*Marjorie Kinnan Rawlings (left), Zora Neale Hurston (right)*

a talent for bringing the unique beauty of Florida to life on the page. The main difference in their works was that while Marjorie wrote about poor whites, Zora wrote about the disenfranchised black community.

Following the college event, Marjorie invited Zora to her husband's hotel for tea. Though seemingly a simple request, this invitation proved complicated due to the prevalence of racism and segregation in the South. According to an eye-witness account, Zora arrived for tea through the back stairs to avoid the scandal she would've caused if she'd gone through the main lobby. Marjorie later wrote to her friend saying that she felt like a coward for having Hurston enter through the back entrance. But she found Zora as having "a most ingratiating personality, a brilliant mind, and [with a] fundamental wisdom that shames most whites."

This story serves as a metaphor for the friendship between Zora and Marjorie. Their attachment to one another was genuine, but it didn't transcend the racial prejudices of their time. For a decade, the friends wrote a dozen letters to one another, and Zora visited Marjorie a few times at her house. There are accounts where it's stated that Zora slept in a separate quarter, where the black help slept. But in a letter from Marjorie to her husband, she wrote that Zora slept inside the house. Which of these is true? Most likely, both are. It's possible that Zora started off sleeping in the maids' chambers, but as the friends got closer and

Marjorie's deeply ingrained, normalized racism wore down, those sleeping arrangements changed.

It can be difficult and even uncomfortable to think of a friendship like this—in which inequality is simply imbedded in the pair's dynamic—as *true* friendship. In letters to other friends, Marjorie admits she didn't want to be publicly associated with Zora, but also acknowledged her inability to fully embrace Zora as cowardly.

Despite the obviously awkward aspects of their relationship, Zora and Marjorie deeply respected one another's work. That's why Zora invited Marjorie to speak at the college to begin with, and why Marjorie later endorsed Zora's work to her editor. These writers were able to develop a closeness within the confines of pervasive racism, and enjoyed one another at least within this context.

I would be so glad to come and take everything off your hands until you are through with your [book]. I know just what you need. . . . Really now, Miss Rawlings, if you find yourself losing your stride, let me help you out. I know so tragically what it means to be trying to concentrate and being nagged by the necessity of living.

–ZORA NEALE HURSTON in a letter to
MARJORIE KINNAN RAWLINGS

... **Zora Neale Hurston has done one of the most beautiful things I have ever known.... I shed tears over this woman's offer. She is an artist in her own right.**

—MARJORIE KINNAN RAWLINGS
in a letter to her husband

# Marilyn
## MONROE
# & Ella
### FITZGERALD

Marilyn Monroe and Ella Fitzgerald met during a time when the racial divide in America meant that black performers were often banned from certain establishments. Ella spent the first part of her career playing in small jazz clubs, and even when she achieved some commercial success in the late 1930s, the notable places would not host her. All of this changed sometime in the '50s, when Marilyn got wind that Ella had been turned down by the Mocambo—one of the hottest nightclubs in Hollywood—because of the color of her skin.

*Marilyn Monroe (left), Ella Fitzgerald (right)*

At the time, Marilyn was well into her career as an actress, but was feeling a bit jaded by the industry, especially after being constantly cast in roles as the "sexy woman" and the object of desire. She decided to take a break, and during her hiatus, she took an interest in jazz and soon became immersed in the world. It was during this time that Marilyn first stumbled upon and fell in love with Ella Fitzgerald, whose voice and musicality Marilyn wished she could emulate. It was rumored that a vocal coach told Monroe to listen to Ella's recording of Gershwin music one hundred times in a row. So, when Marilyn found out her favorite singer was not allowed to perform, she called the manager at the Mocambo and made him a deal: if he booked Ella, then Marilyn promised to sit at a front table every night of the week. It was an offer the manager couldn't refuse. He knew that Marilyn's star power would generate great publicity for his club.

Sure enough, the night was a win-win-win for everyone. The club was abuzz with media, Marilyn got to watch her musician role model perform, and Ella Fitzgerald—propelled into the limelight—never had to sing at a second-rate club again.

The two women remained friends until Marilyn's death in 1962, but there isn't much literature on their relationship beyond this initial meeting. Marilyn's legacy, which still persists today, is her persona both on and off camera. She is known for being a great actress, a sex icon, and last of all, in the eyes of many women, a figure of vulnerability. She let the public in on her thoughts and had definitive stances on such things as romance and womanhood. Despite her bright personality, she was in poor mental health in the years leading up to her death.

Ella, who passed away at seventy-nine in her Beverly Hills home, lived a much longer life. By the end of her career, she had won thirteen Grammys, and received both the National Medal of Arts and the Presidential Medal of Freedom. She collaborated with musical legends Duke Ellington, Frank Sinatra, and Louis Armstrong, and earned the nicknames "Queen of Jazz" and "First Lady of Song" for her smooth, tonally pure sound and impeccable diction. She would always have her friend Marilyn to thank for opening that first door into fame, allowing Ella to prove her worth to the world—worth that Marilyn had noticed from the very beginning.

[Marilyn] was an unusual woman—a little ahead of her times. And she didn't know it.

—ELLA FITZGERALD

# My very favorite person, and I love her as a person as well as a singer. I think she's the greatest, and it's Ella Fitzgerald.

**–MARILYN MONROE**

# Carol & Lucille

BURNETT

BALL

Television icons Carol Burnett and Lucille Ball met for the first time backstage after Carol's off-Broadway show, *Once Upon a Mattress*. Carol was totally starstruck; she was just starting to hit her stride in her career, and the star of *I Love Lucy* had attended her performance! During their half-hour conversation, Lucille called Carol "kid" (Lucille was twenty-two years older), and told Carol she could reach out if she ever needed a favor.

*Carol Burnett (left), Lucille Ball (right)*

And that's exactly what Carol did when, a few years later, CBS said they'd let her do a comedy special if she could get a big name to perform with her. Carol was nervous about asking Lucille, but ultimately thought, *What's the worst that could happen?* Lucille could say no, but it still couldn't hurt to ask. As it turned out, Carol's nerves were for nothing; before she could even formally state her request, Lucille cut to the chase and said, "When do you want me?" From then on, the two women shared a deep bond, and would remain close until Lucille died at age seventy-seven.

Following the special on CBS, Lucille regularly appeared on the first few seasons of *The Carol Burnett Show*, a sketch comedy show that aired for eleven seasons, from 1967 to 1978. Like Lucille, whose show *I Love Lucy* ran from 1951 to 1957, Carol was one of the most popular comedians on television. This was a major feat, as it was especially hard for female comedians to be recognized and taken seriously in the '70s. Carol's producers had even tried to convince Carol to do a sitcom instead, believing that sketch comedy was only for men.

Actress and comedian Tina Fey has cited Carol as one of her role models, someone who proved to her that women belonged in the world of comedy. There is perhaps a parallel to be drawn here between the legacy that Carol passed down to Tina's generation and the one Carol's generation received from Lucille. In *I Love Lucy*, Lucille played an ambitious young woman (named after herself) striving for stardom and always ending up in hilarious trouble. Lucille had impeccable comedic timing and a mean pantomime, but ultimately what charmed audiences was the energy that Lucille brought to slapstick comedy. The show, which won five Emmy Awards among numerous nominations, would become the prototype for family sitcoms for years to come.

Although Carol's show never fermented into a classic the way that *I Love Lucy* did, *The Carol Burnett Show* was equally beloved in its day. It won twenty-five Emmys out of seventy nominations, in addition to nine Golden Globes. In 2013, Carol was awarded the Mark Twain Prize for American Humor, one of the most prestigious honors bestowed upon comedians, and in 2015, she received a Life Achievement Award from the Screen Actors Guild. As part of her acceptance speech, Carol recounted her friendship with Lucille, telling how they met and of the fun baby shower that Lucille threw for her. Carol ended this part of her speech by recalling a touching tradition the friends shared. Lucille would send Carol flowers every year on her birthday. On April 26, 1989, Lucille passed away. It was Carol's birthday. That afternoon, Carol received flowers from her friend for the very last time, with a card that said, "Happy birthday, kid."

Just as [Lucille] was leaving, [she] said, "Kid, if you ever need me for anything, give me a call."

–CAROL BURNETT on first meeting LUCILLE BALL

# Gloria & Dorothy

STEINEM

PITMAN HUGHES

In 1971, a photograph of two women with raised fists and stern faces appeared in *Esquire* magazine. The women were none other than Gloria Steinem and Dorothy Pitman Hughes, and today, this photo remains an iconic representation of female empowerment.

Gloria and Dorothy met in New York while Gloria, an established and prominent leader of the feminist movement, was interviewing Dorothy for a story. Dorothy, who had been involved in the civil rights movement, was working to

*Gloria Steinem (left), Dorothy Pitman Hughes (right)*

improve child welfare. She ran low-cost daycare centers and had started a summer job program for teens. Connecting on their shared passion for justice and equality, the two women talked and talked, and at the end of their conversation, Gloria asked Dorothy if she wanted to come on the road with her and Dorothy said yes! For years the friends toured the country, giving lectures on feminism, racial equality, classism, justice, and freedom. Together, they founded *Ms.* magazine, a feminist magazine that explored sexual harassment, misrepresentations of women's bodies by the media, and abortion, among other hard-hitting subjects that most women's magazines at the time shied away from. The first stand-alone issue was published in 1972 and sold out in a little over a week. The magazine still exists online and in print today.

The understated power of the *Esquire* photo lies in the message of intersectionalism and how it is inherent in feminism. The photo portrays one of Gloria's core beliefs: that black women started the feminist movement and that a lot of what she learned about feminism, she learned from black women. In fact, the raised-fist pose was a nod to the black-power salute of Tommie Smith and John Carlos, track stars at the 1968 Olympics.

In 2014, a year after Gloria won the Presidential Medal of Freedom and more than forty years after the original photo was taken, Gloria and Dorothy got together to recreate this image. This time, at seventy-nine and eighty-two, respectively, Gloria and Dorothy raised their fists to advocate for the beauty of womanhood in old age, adding yet another layer to the message of female empowerment. In the new photo, they look every bit as powerful and radiant as they did in their youth, and the small smiles on their faces—absent in the original—express triumph.

Today, Gloria and Dorothy continue to empower and inspire. Dorothy has initiated many projects in Jacksonville, Florida, (where she now lives) to promote community wellness. At the Women's March on Washington, D.C., Gloria's mere presence served as a reminder that while there's still so much progress to be made, if we're willing to put in the work, we can do it, because look how far we've already come.

I think that
we know that [when]
we're in a jam, we'll
help each other. And
it's the best kind
of family.

–GLORIA STEINEM

We're real sisters. It's not the sisters that were born together, or in the same place, but we know that we can depend on each other.

–DOROTHY PITMAN HUGHES

# Angela
DAVIS
# & Toni
MORRISON

Unbeknownst to many, before Toni Morrison became known as one of the most influential writers of our time, she was an editor at Random House. For twenty years, she worked in publishing, championing black writers so that black experiences could be reflected in literature. She published books by Muhammad Ali, Henry Dumas, Huey P. Newton, and last but not least, educator and activist Angela Davis, who would thenceforth become her lifelong friend.

*Toni Morrison (left), Angela Davis (right)*

Born and raised in Birmingham, Alabama, Angela's world-view was informed by the pervasive racism that she grew up in. The injustices she experienced and bore witness to as a child and teenager (she knew many of the girls killed in the 1963 Birmingham church bombing) drove her to political activism. As a young adult, Angela was a member of the Black Panthers as well as an all-black branch of the Communist party—and was met with opposition for being affiliated with these radical organizations. The administration at UCLA where Angela had been teaching at the time tried to fire her due to these ties, but Angela ended up leaving of her own volition. In 1970, Angela helped in the failed escape of George Jackson, a black radical whom many believe was scapegoated for the death of a prison guard. After serving jail time, Angela was acquitted in 1972.

All of this took place before Angela turned thirty, so when Toni approached Angela with the idea of writing an autobiography, Angela was resistant. She thought it was silly for someone so young to write an autobiography, but moreover, Angela did not want to portray herself as a hero, as is common in autobiographies. It took Toni assuring Angela that she had complete autonomy over her own story to convince Angela to write about her life. True to her promise, Toni never told Angela what or how to write. She instead asked prompting questions that gently pushed Angela toward a stronger manuscript. The autobiography was published in 1974, after which the friends went on tour together to promote the book. (As an aside, it's important to mention that in 1972, Toni wrote a *scathing* review in the *New York Times* of a biography of Angela that was written by a white woman. Toni criticized the author for misrepresenting Angela's life, and called the author "another simpatico white girl who felt she was privy to the secret of how black revolutionaries got that way." The mark of a good editor and friend!)

Toni's own activism lives in her writing, namely in her fiction. Her first novel, *The Bluest Eye*, was published in 1970 when Toni was thirty-nine, and since then, she has written many more. Her two best-known works are *Song of Solomon* (1977), about an African American man who lives in Michigan, and *Beloved* (1987), about an escaped female slave, for which Toni won the Pulitzer Prize. Both titles are now considered classics. Toni received the Presidential Medal of Freedom from Barack Obama in 2012. Like Angela, Toni's worldview was also shaped by her experiences as a black woman, and she has made it a point in her fiction to write from an authentic place, not to appease a white audience. Her characters are good yet often grotesque, complicated and never sentimental, exhibiting a wide range of human tendencies, characteristics, and emotions. Angela, who now teaches at UC Santa Cruz, says that through her writing, Toni has accomplished what every political activist sets out to do: penetrate the collective consciousness and alter the way society thinks about freedom.

I think we would be living in a very different world had we not experienced the impact of Toni Morrison's writing. There is no doubt about the extent to which she has influenced the literary world, not only in this country but all over. She has actually changed the face of the planet. And I see her as a person who made a conscious decision to use her literary talent to bring new ideas into the world, to change the world, absolutely.

—ANGELA DAVIS

**Working with Angela was *sui generis* . . .**

–TONI MORRISON

# Martina

NAVRATILOVA

# &Chris

EVERT

Besides sister-competitors Venus and Serena Williams, there is no better example of sportsmanship than the rivalry between Martina Navratilova and Chris Evert. In sixteen years, the tennis legends played each other eighty times total. Sixty of those matches were finals. The record stands at 43–37, in favor of Martina.

Chris and Martina met in the spring of 1973, at ages eighteen and sixteen, respectively, at a tournament in Akron, Ohio. Before that, Chris made her Grand Slam debut in

*Chris Evert (left), Martina Navratilova (right)*

1971, where she was defeated by Billie Jean King in the semifinals. Martina, who was from Czechoslovakia (now the Czech Republic), was less well-known and was struggling to play in the United States because of her ties to her native country. Two years later, Martina would ask the United States to grant her political asylum.

Since their first meeting—where Chris beat Martina in two sets—the two women have been close friends and have managed to stay above the media's attempts to pit them against one another. Blond and thin, Chris was adored by fans as the all-American girl next door. The media focused their attentions on her beauty and chose to ignore her tough and competitive on-court demeanor. Even her moniker, "the Ice Maiden," seemed like an attempt to make her seem fierce but not *too* aggressive. As her rival, Martina was thus portrayed as the complete opposite; where Chris was depicted as feminine and dainty, Martina was criticized for being masculine and volatile. Like Chris, Martina was an intense tennis player, but the media's ridicule was largely fueled by Martina's liberal politics, about which she was very outspoken. She openly advocated for women's rights, environmentalism, and animal rights.

Obsessed with this rivalry, fans polarized the two athletes by calling themselves "Chrissie fans" or "Martina fans." But Chris and Martina never let this affect their friendship. They were each other's biggest supporters. When Martina came out as bisexual in 1981, Chris was one of the first to stick up for her. She has said that Martina's boldness inspired her to climb out of the "good girl" pigeonhole that the media placed her into.

In the summer of 1986, Chris and Martina played for the United States Fed Cup team in Czechoslovakia. It was an emotional moment for Martina, who had received asylum and had not returned to her home country in eleven years. Chris put her arm around Martina as she cried during the Czech national anthem. When Chris was in low spirits following her divorce in 1987, Martina invited her on a ski trip to Aspen and introduced her to a skier named Andy Mill. Martina let Chris and Andy borrow her bedroom on that trip, and as fate would have it, the two fell in love and got married in 1990.

But perhaps the most incredible feat of this friendship is how they were able to separate their personal and professional lives. Chris and Martina showed each other no mercy when it came to tennis, and both name their greatest victories as the matches they won against each other. After losing to Chris for years, Martina finally won her first Wimbledon in 1978 against Chris, and said it was the most important victory of her career because she knew then that she could be the best. Chris has said that her most satisfying win was against Martina at the 1985 French Open, a victory that put an end to Martina's two-year winning streak. At the end of their careers, each had amassed eighteen Grand Slam singles titles, and Martina a record nine at Wimbledon.

We've been through so much history, so many layers of emotions. We were such opposites, it enabled us to get closer. She has my back; I have hers. I think people forget that we were left alone in the locker room every Sunday after we played final matches, and one of us would be crying and the other would be comforting— nobody saw that.

—CHRIS EVERT

We brought out the best in each other. It's almost not right to say who's better. If you tried to make the perfect rivalry, we were it.

**–MARTINA NAVRATILOVA**

# Oprah & Gayle
WINFREY

KING

Oprah Winfrey and Gayle King first met at a news station in Baltimore. They were both in their early twenties and just launching their careers. Oprah was a news anchor and Gayle was a production assistant, and there weren't too many chances for them to interact on set in these roles. But one fateful winter night, Gayle slept over at Oprah's place due to a snowstorm. Trapped inside, the two young women talked all night and found they shared many similarities.

*Oprah Winfrey (top), Gayle King (bottom)*

Although they came from different upbringings—Gayle was raised in an upper-middle-class family, while Oprah grew up poor—they found common ground in their experiences as ambitious black women. Growing up, they often felt like they didn't fit into people's assumptions of what a black woman should be. They enjoyed Neil Diamond and Barry Manilow. They agreed that being smart and articulate were things to be proud of, and in this shared philosophy, they were able to see themselves in each other.

Four decades later, Gayle is now the co-host of *CBS This Morning* and Oprah is a media tycoon, known for her work as a talk show host, actress, producer, and humanitarian. Oprah has won numerous awards, and has been featured in *Time*'s list of most influential people *ten* times.

Needless to say, a lot has changed in these women's lives since they met. They are a whole lot richer and more well-known now, but their friendship has always remained the same. Gayle is currently the editor-at-large of *O, The Oprah Magazine*, and was also a correspondent on *The Oprah Winfrey Show*, which won forty-seven Daytime Emmys in the twenty-five years that it aired, from 1986 to 2011. But their professional relationship just barely scratches the surface. The friends call each other at least once a day, every day. After Gayle gave birth to her second child, Oprah gifted her bestie a full-time nanny to help Gayle take care of her children for as long as she needed. The nanny ended up staying for seven years. In Oprah's house, there is an entire wing dedicated to Gayle.

These two best friends are also known to joke around with one another. In December 2016, while Gayle was on *CBS This Morning*, Oprah texted Gayle's assistant, "plz tell Gayle I'm on treadmill & it's hard to focus w/the circus around your neck." The colorful necklace was admittedly hugely oversized, and Gayle reacted to Oprah's diss the way any true best friend would—by putting Oprah on blast via social media. On Instagram, Gayle posted a picture of herself wearing the necklace with Oprah's scathing text in the caption.

These two women are the epitome of "best friends forever." Oprah and Gayle have referred to one another as soul mates, and for those of us who've experienced a similar friendship, we know that this kind of love is often truer than any romance could be.

Something about this relation-ship feels otherworldly to me, like it was designed by a power and a hand greater than my own. Whatever this friendship is, it's been a very fun ride—and we've taken it together.

—OPRAH WINFREY

I see myself in Oprah's light, not in her shadow. Who doesn't want to be her best friend? There's no downside. We've been friends since we were twenty-one and twenty-two and we're now sixty-one and sixty-two. I never think, 'Oh, wow, people just see me as Oprah's best friend.' Anyone who knows me doesn't see me that way. I'm like, 'Yes, I am her best friend—how do you do?' I don't run away from that.

—GAYLE KING

# Lily &
TOMLIN
# Jane
FONDA

Watch any scene from the movie *9 to 5* and you'll be charmed by the humor and candor that these women emanate—mostly off their tremendous '80s blowouts. In this feel-good revenge comedy, comedian Lily Tomlin and long-time actress Jane Fonda expose the sexist environment of the office, forcing audiences to recognize the commonplace prejudices that women endure daily. The basic premise of the movie is this: a misogynistic, brutish, uncaring male boss tortures his female employees (played by Lily, Jane, and Dolly Parton), until one day, the

*Lily Tomlin (left), Jane Fonda (right)*

women decide they've had enough and take matters into their own hands. Hilarity ensues. The movie came out in 1980, and Lily and Jane have been close friends ever since.

Lily and Jane were each stars in their own right prior to meeting. Lily was a successful comedian and television actress, and had been nominated for an Academy Award for best supporting actress in the film *Nashville*. Jane, meanwhile, was practically a household name in Hollywood. Her most-acclaimed films include *They Shoot Horses, Don't They?*, *Klute*, and *Coming Home*. She won the Academy Award for best actress for the last two.

Even though they had known of each other for a long time, the first time they met was when Jane attended Lily's comedy show. Jane knew after watching Lily's performance that she was perfect for *9 to 5*—but at first, Lily said no to the project! It took Jane a year to persuade Lily to get on board.

Fast forward almost forty years and many, many awards later—and the friends are still fighting against female prejudice on the screen. Their current show, *Grace and Frankie*, explores womanhood in a different context, one that's been largely overlooked in television: old age. Their characters, Grace (Jane) and Frankie (Lily), develop a close yet complicated bond after their husbands leave them in order to be with one another. The show dispels ageist assumptions that older people—older women in particular—don't crave love or sex; that this piece of their humanity has somehow, over time, worn off. This is certainly not the case for Grace and Frankie, who talk about their sex drives and desires for affection. In the show, they even start a business selling vibrators.

Lily and Jane further dispel stereotypes of older women by just being themselves. In March 2017, they flashed their Planned Parenthood pins on *The Late Show with Stephen Colbert*, and in a similar vein, dissed President Trump and proudly announced their participation in the Los Angeles Women's March. Together they celebrated Jane's birthday by participating in a Standing Rock protest. They're letting the world know that being a woman at any age is active, evolving, meaningful—and also a whole lot of fun.

**We're friends because I just love her. I know Jane has my back whenever she can.**

–LILY TOMLIN

# Women's friendships are like a renewable source of power.

**–JANE FONDA**

# Anna & Grace

WINTOUR

CODDINGTON

Fashion icons Anna Wintour and Grace Coddington's relationship is proof that friends don't necessarily have to be similar in order to be compatible. Often described as yin and yang, Anna and Grace are, in many ways, the total opposite of each other.

They arrived at American *Vogue* the same year: 1988; Anna as editor in chief and Grace as creative director. They were highly qualified for these positions, with long careers in fashion editorial that eventually led them to *Vogue*. Anna

*Anna Wintour (left), Grace Coddington (right)*

started off as an editorial assistant with *Harper's Bazaar UK* and eventually transitioned to the American edition. From there, she worked at *Viva*, *New York Magazine*, and *House & Garden*, before finally joining American *Vogue*. Meanwhile, Grace, after a successful modeling career, worked at British *Vogue* for nineteen years. She then moved to the United States to work for Calvin Klein before ending up at American *Vogue*.

For thirty years, Anne and Grace worked together in the same roles they started in. Anna made business decisions and served as a visible face of *Vogue*—one perpetually framed in a sleek bob with straight-across bangs, half-hidden behind huge sunglasses. Meanwhile, Grace was in charge of the behind-the-scenes work, which included styling and overseeing shoots with the industry's top photographers. Their roles suited them perfectly, and perhaps, also, these roles reflected their opposite views on fashion. For Anna, fashion was about entertainment and trends, whereas for Grace, fashion was supposed to be, first and foremost, about art. For this bygone sentiment, Grace has been perceived as a sort of moral underdog in an industry that many believe has slipped into the depths of vanity and consumerism.

Anna embraced the celebrity culture that has now merged with the fashion world, while Grace resisted it. Grace preferred that fashion and Hollywood remain separate, and advocated using models in shoots as opposed to using celebrities. The contrast between Anna and Grace is evident even in their personal styles. Anna loves furs and accessories. Grace does not. Anna detests black, so much so, that everyone knows not to wear it at her events. Grace loves black, deeming it a most forgiving color, and wears tons of it—even in front of Anna.

The intimidating effect that Anna has on most people never fazed Grace, who is known to be one of the few people who could speak to Anna as an equal. Because of this and the complementary differences between them, Anna and Grace worked extremely well together and shared in *Vogue*'s success throughout the years. In 2016, at the age of seventy-four, Grace stepped down from her position and is now working on personal projects related to fashion. Anna rose again to mogul status in 2013, when she was promoted to artistic director of Condé Nast, the publisher that oversees *Vogue* and twenty other titles, including *Bon Appétit*, *Pitchfork*, and *The New Yorker*.

R.J. Cutler, the director of *The September Issue* documentary, said about them: "Though I don't think of them at all as rivals, in thinking of Anna and Grace's relationship, I was reminded of what McEnroe said about Borg, which is that if Borg hadn't retired early, he would've been a much better tennis player and a better human being. I do think these women bring each other to new heights."

There's such a sense of positivity to what [Grace] does. She's never subscribed to, you know, angst and worry in her shoots. I feel that there's a lightness to them— a sense of hope.

—ANNA WINTOUR

I'm not the 'anti-Anna.' The smarter people can see it's not a question of fighting. It's how we work together. She can't just say yes to everything. I certainly don't. I just have a different way of saying no.

—GRACE CODDINGTON

# Michelle & Valerie

**OBAMA**

**JARRETT**

Not only did the friendship between Michelle Obama and Valerie Jarrett greatly impact their own careers, as they built each other up and created opportunities for one another; their friendship also benefited Michelle's husband, former president Barack Obama. It all began in 1991, in Chicago, when Valerie offered Michelle a job at city hall. Valerie served as chief of staff to the mayor at the time, and was well-established in the Chicago political scene. After meeting Michelle's then fiancé Barack Obama, she introduced the two young lawyers to her inner circle, many of

*Michelle Obama (left), Valerie Jarrett (right)*

whom ended up supporting Barack in his journey to the White House.

During those early years, Valerie was a mentor to both Michelle and Barack; the couple confided in Valerie about their dreams and ambitions. This level of intimacy gave Valerie a unique role in Barack's ascent to the presidency. Michelle and Barack trusted Valerie, so they asked her to drive a large part of Barack's presidential campaign. She proved instrumental in helping Barack win the trust of reluctant voters and black leaders, and advised Barack in major decisions. After he won the election, Valerie was named senior adviser, and though many were skeptical of this appointment—they thought appointing a hometown buddy to such an important seat showed flawed judgment on the part of the new president—Valerie stayed in this role for both terms. She helped the Obamas transition into the White House in 2008, and then helped them transition out of it in 2017. For eight years, she devoted herself to the president by aiding Barack in crucial matters such as selecting the cabinet, preserving and maintaining his image, and corresponding with leaders across the country. It was Valerie who called Barack in 2015 to share the exciting news that they'd won the Supreme Court case legalizing same-sex marriage.

But Valerie was more to Michelle and Barack than just a means to getting a leg up on the career ladder. She is also one of their closest friends and has been a part of their lives for nearly thirty years. She was called "the Night Stalker" by some in the White House because she chatted with the Obamas after work hours in their private quarters. Whenever the former president gave a speech, Valerie could be spotted sitting in the audience next to Michelle, looking up at Barack with such awe and admiration. Barack has said he can't look at Valerie while speaking for fear that he might break down in tears.

Valerie has also gone by another moniker—"First Friend." She's gone on vacation with the Obamas to Hawaii and Martha's Vineyard. Michelle has referred to Valerie as both a mother and a big sister, and Valerie has said that Michelle and Barack are like the siblings she never had. Interestingly, right after Barack's first win, there was some post-election buzz about whether or not Valerie would try and take Barack's old Senate seat. It was then that Michelle took action, expressing to Valerie how badly she wanted her to remain close by in D.C., where she would be a great comfort and aid to Barack during his presidency. In the end, as we know, Valerie trusted Michelle and took herself out of the running. Somehow, the White House doesn't seem too shabby an alternative.

**[Michelle's]
at the
top of her
game. She's
fabulous
at fifty.**

–VALERIE JARRETT

I can count on someone like Valerie to take my hand and say, 'You need to think about these three things.' Like a mom, a big sister, I trust her implicitly.

–MICHELLE OBAMA

# Tina & Amy
### FEY
### POEHLER

Before they became household names, Tina Fey and Amy Poehler were struggling comedians trying to make it in the Chicago comedy scene. They met at the Improv-Olympic (now iO) Theater in 1993 and were instantly inseparable. They later joined renowned comedy companies Second City and the Upright Citizens Brigade (UCB), where they continued performing together.

In 1997 Tina's career took her to New York City, where she worked as a writer and performer on *Saturday Night Live*

*Tina Fey (top), Amy Poehler (bottom)*

(the dream!). For years, Tina asked Amy to join *SNL*, but Amy was devoted to UCB Chicago and kept turning down the offer. It wasn't until 2001 that Amy joined *SNL* and the friends were finally reunited. Together they hosted "Weekend Update" and famously portrayed Katie Couric (Amy) and Sarah Palin (Tina) during the 2008 presidential election. Since *SNL*, Tina and Amy have worked on many projects together, including hit movies *Mean Girls*, *Baby Mama*, and *Sisters*. The hilarious duo also had the special honor of hosting the Golden Globes three years in a row from 2013-2015, a sidesplitting treat for viewers both at home and in the audience.

Despite much of their careers being intertwined, Tina and Amy have also achieved their own personal success. After *SNL*, they both went on to produce and become lead actresses on their own TV shows—*30 Rock* (Fey) and *Parks and Recreation* (Poehler). Both have won Emmys, Golden Globes, and numerous other awards for their acting, writing, and producing.

Off screen, these ladies have a very close relationship. Tina even had her character on *30 Rock* keep a picture of Amy in her office. They've both dedicated a chapter to the other in their autobiographical books, and they joke about marrying their children to one another. "I don't care if it's a girl or a boy," Poehler said while pregnant with her son Archie. "I want it to marry Alice Richmond, Tina's daughter. We'd make a lovely mother and mother-in-law of the bride."

From humble beginnings to becoming comedy legends, Tina and Amy have seen each other through it all. In what has mostly been viewed as a boys' club, these ladies didn't knock each other down in order to secure a place in comedy. Instead, they made room for each other to shine as individuals while also reaping the rewards of working together. Also? They proved beyond all reasonable doubt that women *are* funny. *Twist!*

I think one of your [Tina's] greatest accomplishments was transitioning from the captain you were at *SNL* to creating a show [*30 Rock*]. That is so hard—extricating yourself from a place you were so comfortable and successful, then doing something so well. That, and the fact you invented the word *flerm.*

—AMY POEHLER

I would say that
one of your greatest
accomplishments,
Amy Poehler,
is that you have so
successfully used your
art and comedy as a
source of positivity
in the world.

**–TINA FEY**

# Aaliyah & Missy

ELLIOTT

At age fourteen, Aaliyah released her first R&B album, *Age Ain't Nothing but a Number*. As though the title were a prophecy, the album became a huge success, selling over five hundred thousand copies worldwide. For her second album, rather than working with more visible producers—following the success of her first record, she had many to choose from—Aaliyah decided to take a risk and collaborate with two lesser-known musicians, whose sounds were more unique and, at the time, more underground. These musicians were none other than Timbaland and Missy

*Aaliyah (left), Missy Elliott (right)*

Elliott. Although they are hip-hop royalty now, back then, Timbaland and Missy had just left a failed record imprint and were collaborating to craft tracks for other musicians.

Missy helped write nine tracks for Aaliyah's sophomore album, *One in a Million*, including the double platinum single "If Your Girl Only Knew." Missy Elliott's sound quickly caught on, and she went on to produce music for some of the hottest acts in the industry, including Ciara, Ginuwine, Beyoncé, and Mary J. Blige, among others. The five-time Grammy winner has also achieved incredible success as a solo artist. Her singles "Get Ur Freak On" and "Work It" are staples at every '90s and aughts-themed party now and for the foreseeable future.

Despite such a promising beginning, Aaliyah's career was sadly cut short when she died in 2001. She was flying back from the Bahamas where she had been filming a music video for the single off her self-titled album, *Aaliyah*, when her plane suddenly crashed. At that year's MTV Video Music Awards, Missy stood up and said, ". . . we're going to keep Aaliyah's legacy alive. I didn't write anything, I just felt like I had to come from the heart. And I love you, Aaliyah, and you're forever missed."

Ten years later, Aaliyah's name was once again the hot topic of conversation in the music world when a posthumous album was set to be released by hip-hop artist Drake. Many were upset by the fact that Drake, who never knew Aaliyah personally, didn't involve Timbaland or Missy Elliott in the album at all. When asked about this in interviews, Missy Elliott gracefully declined to engage in any drama. She said, "I don't even want to talk about that because I'm being asked a lot. It's very sensitive, but because [Aaliyah] represented positive energy. She was positive. I don't ever want to bring controversy around her name." To this day, Missy continues to spread Aaliyah's positive energy and pays homage to her friend. From birthday tweets to concert shout-outs, Missy keeps Aaliyah's memory alive.

She would just do silly stuff. One time, she put these big fake teeth in her mouth, the kind you get at a joke shop, and she came into my room and started doing the scenes from *Romeo Must Die*. Her personality was very playful, but she was also equally caring and compassionate.

–MISSY ELLIOTT

# Williams Sisters

**VENUS & SERENA**

They're two of the most decorated athletes of our time, and their accomplishments are all the more astounding when we recall how their journey began. Venus and Serena Williams grew up in Compton, California, and started playing pretty much as soon as they were able to pick up a racket. Coached by their parents, Venus and Serena practiced every day before and after school. Surrounded by gang violence in their neighborhood, the girls' safety was always an issue—especially when they were outside. This setting seemed like the complete

*Venus (left), Serena (right)*

antithesis of tennis, a sport with a reputation of being rich and white.

But Venus and Serena were disciplined and diligent. They kept practicing their slices, forehands, backhands, and serves. They played their first professional tournaments when they were just in high school, and their careers jetted off from there. Playing together in doubles, they have won fourteen Grand Slam titles and three Olympic gold medals. By 2017, Serena had won twenty-three major singles titles and Venus had won seven (but you can promptly forget these numbers, as they're just going to keep going up).

Now in their mid-thirties, Venus and Serena are praised for their athletic longevity. Few athletes in any sport have stayed in the game for as long as they have, but in addition to that, the sisters persisted through severe debilitating health issues. In 2011, Venus found out she had Sjögren's syndrome, an autoimmune disorder that causes terrible joint pain and fatigue. A year before that, Serena suffered life-threatening blood clots in her lungs, forcing her to sit out for a year. But just when critics were gearing up to write retrospectives on their legendary careers, the sisters made a comeback. In 2012, Serena won Wimbledon (again, her fifth time) and also the Olympic gold medal in women's singles. Serena and Venus teamed up to take home the gold in women's doubles.

Of course, their relationship isn't all high fives and mid-set hugs—Venus and Serena are frequently rivals on the court. Most recently in January 2017, they faced off at the Australian Open final. It was the ninth Grand Slam final that they'd played against each other, and the seventh that Serena has won. Based on the number of wins, Serena is the proven better player, but if you're looking for a story about cattiness or ill will between the sisters, you won't find one. Venus and Serena are nothing but supportive of one another, and have said that they view a win for one of them as a victory for both.

The sisters are just as close in their personal lives as they are in their profession. As adults, they shared a house together for years, and when Serena finally decided to move out and buy her own house in 2014, she called it "growing up." But the two sisters don't have to travel far to see one another. Serena ended up moving just down the street.

There's no way I would be at 23 [Grand Slams] without her; there's no way I would be at 1 without her. There's no way I would have anything without her. She's my inspiration. She's the only reason I'm standing here today, and the only reason that the Williams sisters exist. So thank you, Venus, for inspiring me to be the best player I could be and inspiring me to work hard.

—SERENA to VENUS after she beat her
in the Australian Open

Congratulations, Serena, on No. 23. I have been there right with you. Some of them I lost right there against you. . . . Your win has always been my win. I think you know that. And all the time I couldn't be there, wouldn't be there, didn't get there, you were there. I'm enormously proud of you. You mean the world to me.

—VENUS to SERENA after losing to her in the finals of the Australian Open

# Abbi
JACOBSON

&

# Ilana
GLAZER

Abbi Jacobson and Ilana Glazer both entered the comedy scene through the Upright Citizens Brigade in New York City. They were the only women in their improv practice group, and both were having a hard time earning spots on the UCB house teams.

Around this time, Abbi was working on her own project with another friend, but after getting some bad reviews, her friend was discouraged and wanted out. When Abbi confided in Ilana about this, Ilana suggested that *they*

*Ilana Glazer (left), Abbi Jacobson (right)*

partner up instead. In no time, the friends began working feverishly on *Broad City*, chronicling the lives of two young women who try to make it in New York City and get caught up in crazy shenanigans along the way. Abbi and Ilana worked sales jobs in order to pay rent and survive in New York, and in their free time, they got together and wrote in coffee shops all around the city. In 2009, the first "season" of *Broad City* debuted on YouTube. It was comprised of two-and-a-half-minute DIY shorts. The poor video quality, terrible lighting, and shaky camera angles made the show feel raw and authentic, and added to its charm. Abbi and Ilana used their names for their characters, who were essentially just exaggerated versions of themselves.

After the first season developed a cult following, the friends decided to add some production value to the second season. They created a schedule and stuck to it, posting a new video every week, and put some PR behind the show. Comedy legend Amy Poehler knew about *Broad City* and was a big fan, so when Abbi and Ilana reached out to her about making an appearance on their show, Amy agreed—and she also agreed to be the show's executive producer. Not surprisingly, her involvement was a huge help. Amy was able to get the show onto Comedy Central, where it expanded into a longer format with half-hour episodes and, of course, got a major upgrade production-wise. The show averaged a little more than a million viewers per episode in its first season, making it one of the highest-rated first seasons of any Comedy Central show.

Abbi and Ilana are currently the it-girls of television, heralded for their fresh, honest, and hilarious depictions of urban life for the millennial generation. They wear their fame so well that no one would guess the amount of hard work and persistence that it took for them to get where they are today. But if you go back and watch the web episodes of *Broad City*, you'll be inspired by how far the two friends have come.

And in each
part of the process—
the writing, the actual
production, the acting, the
editing, even in interviews—
we have found our
strengths and weaknesses,
and often where each of
our weaknesses lie,
the strengths of the other
come through.

**–ABBI JACOBSON**

**And being able
to recognize a weakness
is so much easier when
I have this brilliant partner
who I know can pick up
the slack in an area
I'm weak in—and that's
a strength in itself. It's
fucking fabulous.**

**–ILANA GLAZER**

# Malala & Muzoon

YOUSAFZAI

ALMELLEHAN

Malala Yousafzai's story became known worldwide after she was shot in 2012 by a Taliban gunman when she was only fifteen years old. The terrorist group in Pakistan had been targeting her since she was eleven for speaking out against them in her campaign for girls' education, which the Taliban had sought to take away. Her injuries from the bullet required multiple surgeries; a portion of her skull had to be removed. Malala was eventually relocated to Birmingham, England, in 2013 for further medical attention. Still on the Taliban's hit list, she has lived in Birmingham

*Muzoon Almellehan (left), Malala Yousafzai (right)*

**152**

ever since, but she refuses to be silent. Her campaign for global education has taken her all over the world, to some of the most destitute places, where she continues to spread hope.

Malala and Muzoon's paths crossed for the first time in 2014, while Malala was visiting a refugee camp in Jordan to shine awareness on the plight of Syrian refugees. Muzoon was staying there at the time while the civil war raged on in Syria, a place that had become unsuitable for living. Like Malala, Muzoon was passionate about education, but she could see that not everyone around her recognized its value. The number of child marriages was growing at an alarming rate within the camps due to the popular idea that early marriage was the only way for parents to secure their daughters' futures. Muzoon, whose father had instilled in her a deep love of learning, went door to door in the camp urging parents to keep their daughters in school rather than forcing them into marriage. Muzoon argued that education is one of the only ways for women to improve their lives and protect themselves. For her vigilance, media outlets that picked up on her story called her "the Malala of Syria," a moniker she takes pride in because she so admires the work that Malala does.

In December 2014, Muzoon got to fly to Oslo to watch Malala accept the Nobel Peace Prize. It was a special night. At seventeen, Malala was (she still is) the youngest person to be given the honor. A year later, Muzoon would once again have to relocate—this time to England, where she and her family were given refugee status. Malala was thrilled when she found out that Muzoon would be living so close! Soon after Muzoon and her family arrived in their new home, Malala and her parents visited Muzoon and gave her family a proper welcome.

Having seen and withstood the horrors of war and terrorism, these young activists will stop at nothing in their mission to spread education and advocate for girls' rights. The world waits to see what additional good these friends will accomplish now that they're together.

It was the happiest moment of my life when I heard Muzoon was here because I remember the refugee camp and the situation in which she was living there. Now we can work together.

—MALALA YOUSAFZAI

I'm so proud to be called the "Malala of Syria." Malala's a very dedicated, strong person who faced huge difficulties in her life trying to promote education. So that gives me a huge motivation to do more.

–MUZOON ALMELLEHAN

# Acknowledgments

The quotations used in this publication have been sourced from the following listed titles:

Rare Radio Interview

EllaFitzgerald.com

*Carol Burnett Lifetime Achievement*, SAG Awards 2016

*A Potent Pair: A Q&A with Gloria Steinem and Dorothy Pitman Hughes,* The Times-Union

*Toni Morrison and Angela Davis on Friendship and Creativity,* University of Santa Cruz Newscenter

*The Match Made in Heaven,* The Guardian

*A Winning Friendship,* Parade

*Gayle King Thinks Her Show Can Win Morning Ratings Race,* NY Post

*The O Interview: Gayle and Oprah, Uncensored,* O Magazine

*A Hilarious Celebration of Lifelong Female Friendship,* TED

*Always in Fashion,* New York Times

*Amazing Grace Coddington: Inside the World of US Vogue's Creative Director,* The Guardian

*Turning 50, Michelle Obama Focuses on Final 3-Year Stretch in White House,* Washington Post

*An Old Hometown Mentor, Still at Obama's Side,* New York Times

*Tina Fey's and Amy Poehler's Answers to Fan Questions
Will Make You Love Them Even More Than You Thought
Possible*, Glamour

*Aaliyah: 1979-2001*, Rolling Stones

*Serena Williams Beats Venus Williams to Win Her 7th Australian Open Title*, New York Times

*How Broad City Became the Greatest Show on Television*,
OUT

*Malala and Muzoon Reunited in the UK*, BBC

*'Malala of Syria': The Inspiring Story of One Girl's Fight to
Educate Refugees*, CNN

**VIOLET ZHANG** lives in Bushwick, New York, with three amazing roommates and one sweet kitty named Tofu. She thinks women are smart, hilarious, kind, and capable of all things.

**SALLY NIXON** is an illustrator based in Little Rock, Arkansas. Her clients include *Lenny Letter*, *Neon*, and the *Idle Class*, and her work has been featured by *Vice*, *Bustle*, *Cosmo*, *Bust*, and more.